What Birds Can Teach Us

Inspiring Quotes & Beautiful Images

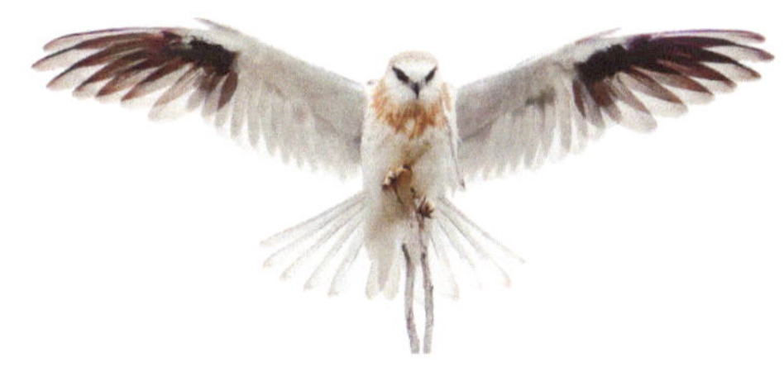

Julie Pallant

For the birds who bring colour and
song to our world, and for the
people who take comfort
in their presence.

Sometimes life feels like it's rushing past us, and we can get caught up in the pressure of everyday demands. In this book I invite you to slow down, take a breath, and let yourself be uplifted by the wonders of nature.

The birds you'll meet in these pages were photographed near my home in Ballina, Australia. Each one carries a message of resilience, grace, and joy. Their presence reminds us that no matter what storms we face, there is always beauty nearby, waiting to lift our spirits.

It is a book to keep on your table for those moments when you need comfort or perspective, and a perfect gift for a friend or family member who could use a little light in their day.

I hope that these pages remind you that, even in the midst of challenges, beauty is always near if you take the time to notice.

Julie Pallant

You don't need size to make an impression — just timing, tone, and a touch of flair.

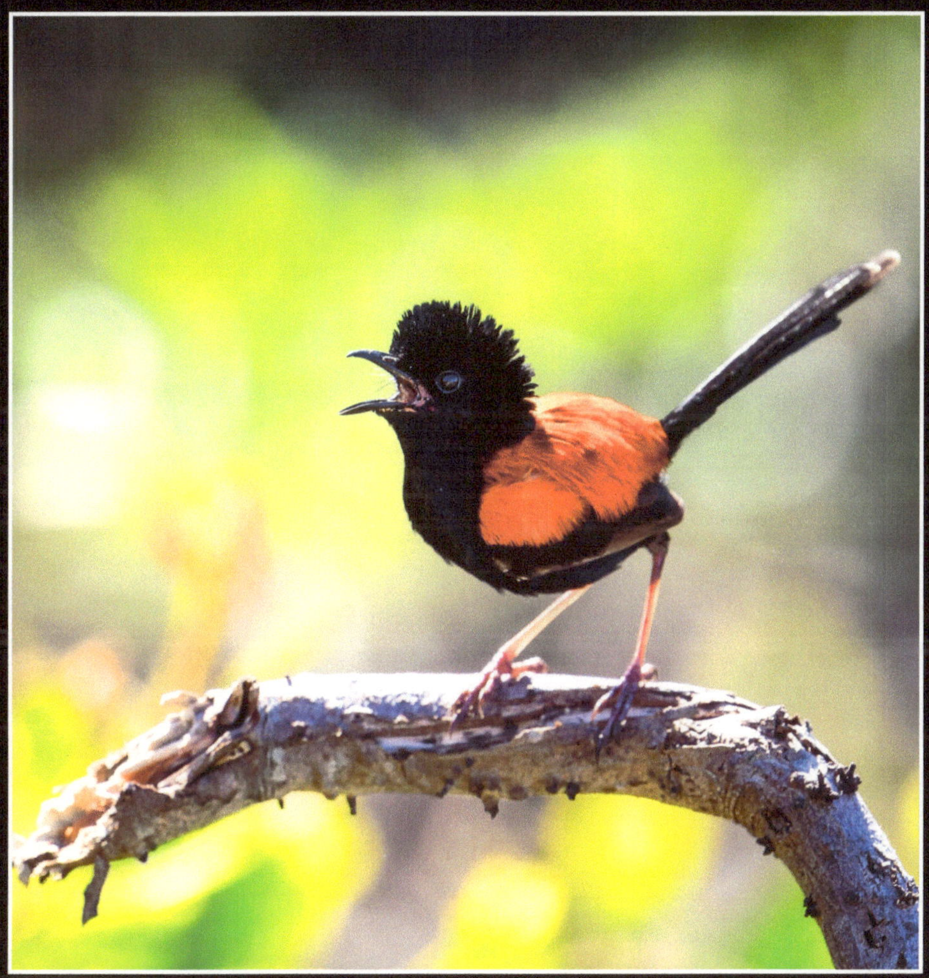

Red-backed Fairywren

True poise is not the absence of struggle—it's the art of moving gracefully while paddling furiously toward your destination.

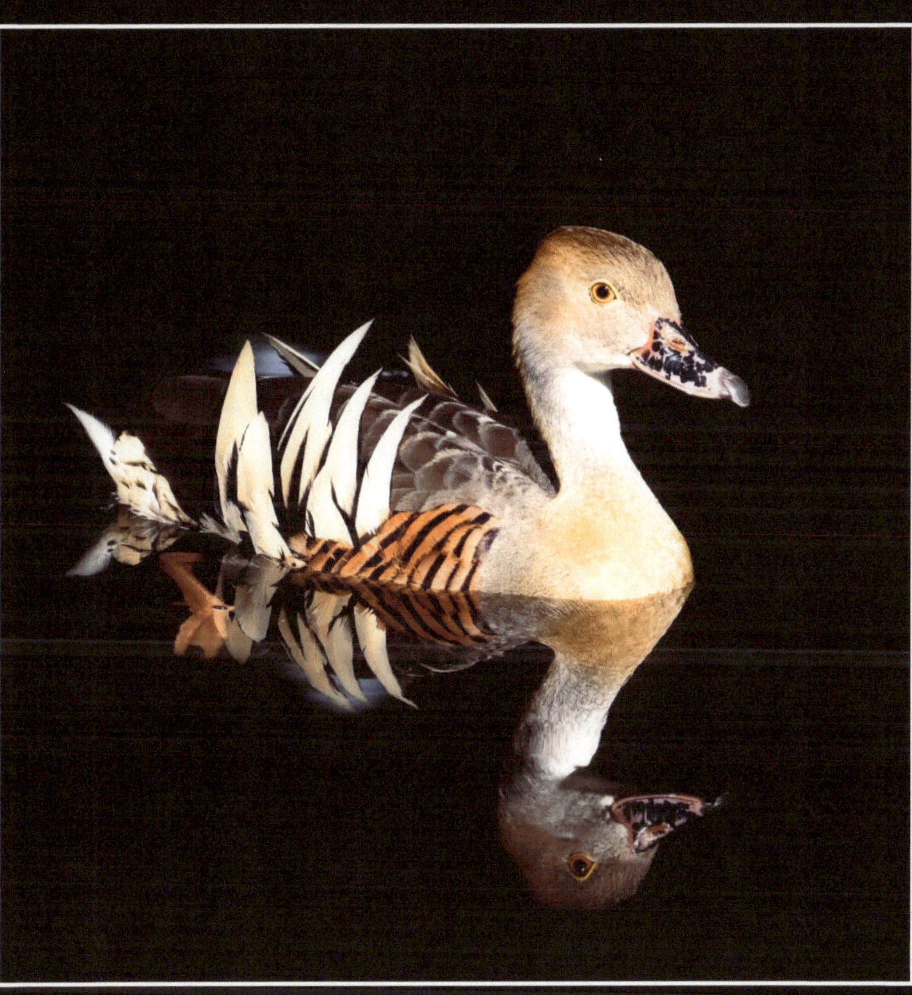

Plumed Whistling Duck

Be still, like the kingfisher.
Let the world move around you,
and when your moment comes,
strike with confidence.

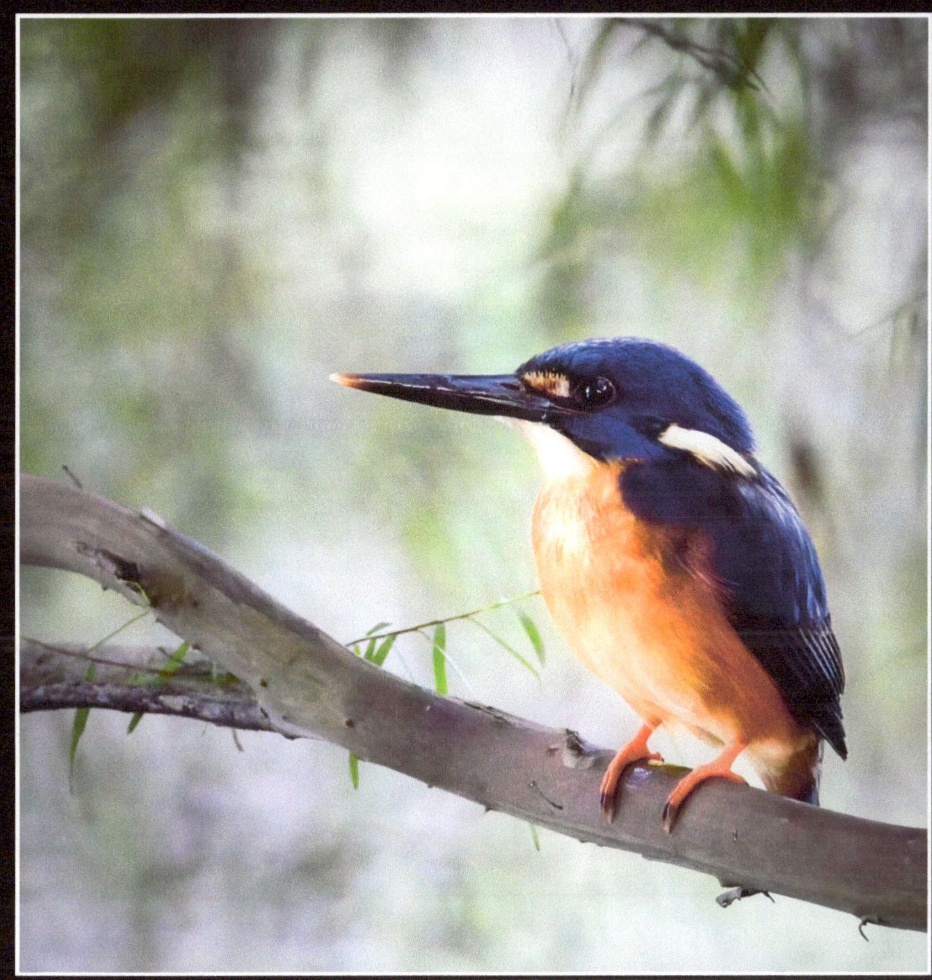

Azure Kingfisher

Calm is not the absence of rain,
but the grace to accept whatever
the day brings.

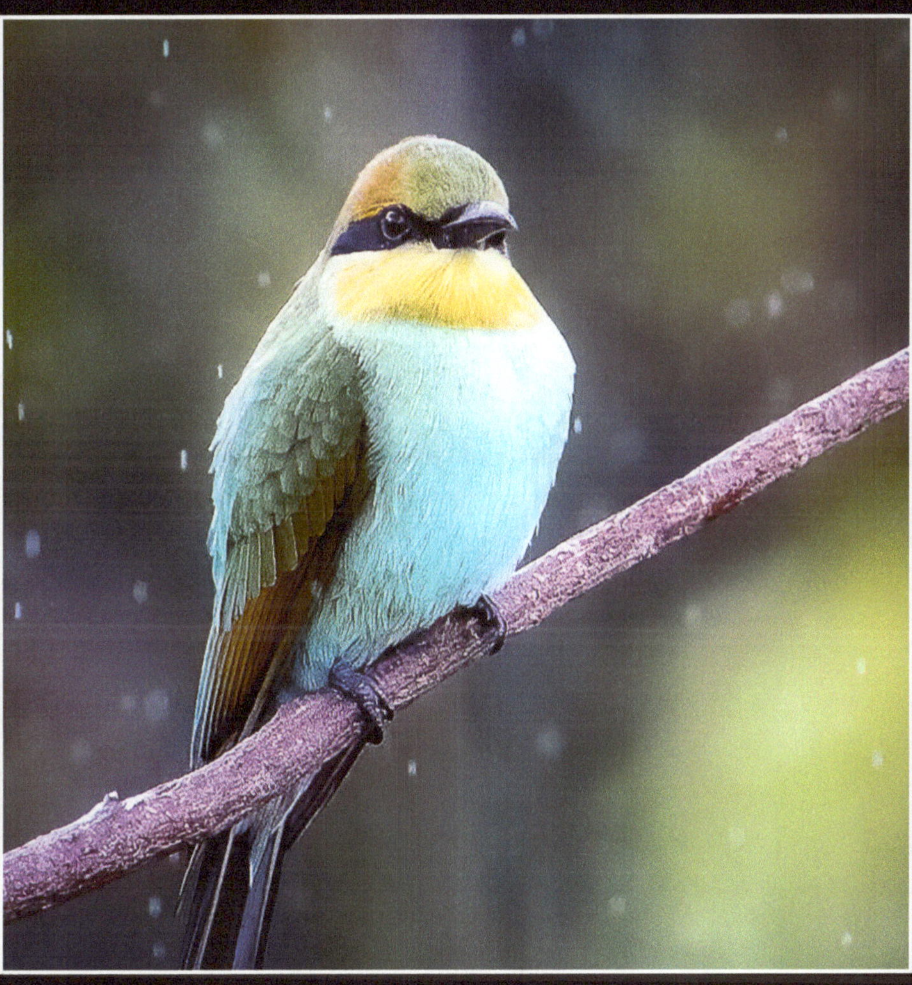

Rainbow Bee-eater (Juvenile)

Watch the birds and learn patience.
Observe the sky and find perspective.
Notice the trees and discover strength.
See the flowers and remember beauty.

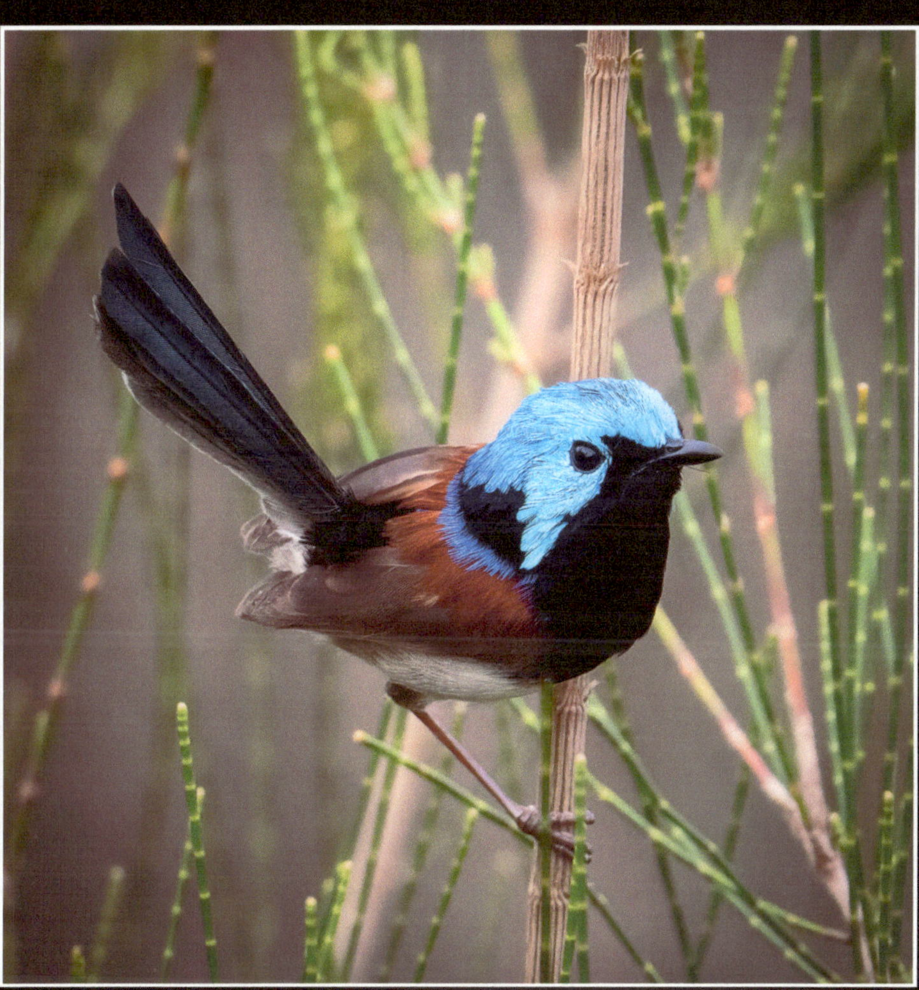

Variegated Fairywren

What if love isn't about finding someone to complete you, but finding someone whose natural rhythm creates perfect balance with your own?

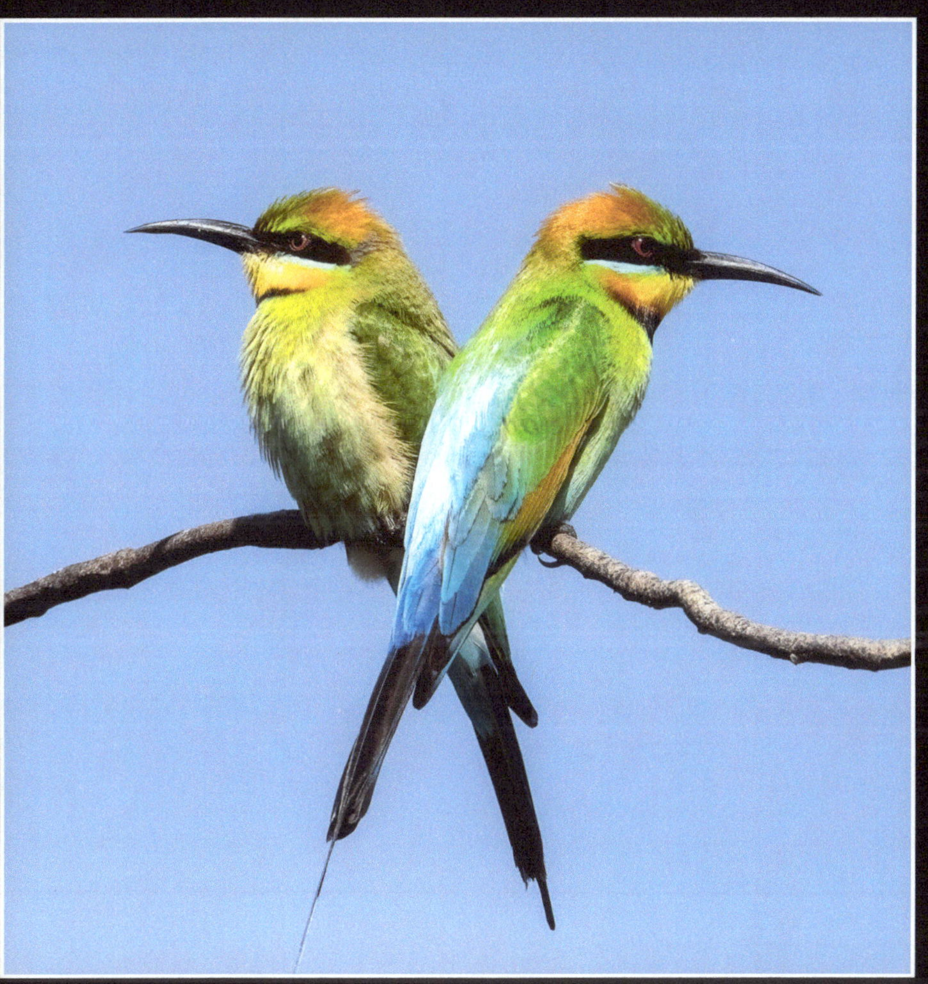

Rainbow Bee-eater

Every day's a good day to dress up
and show the world what
you've got.

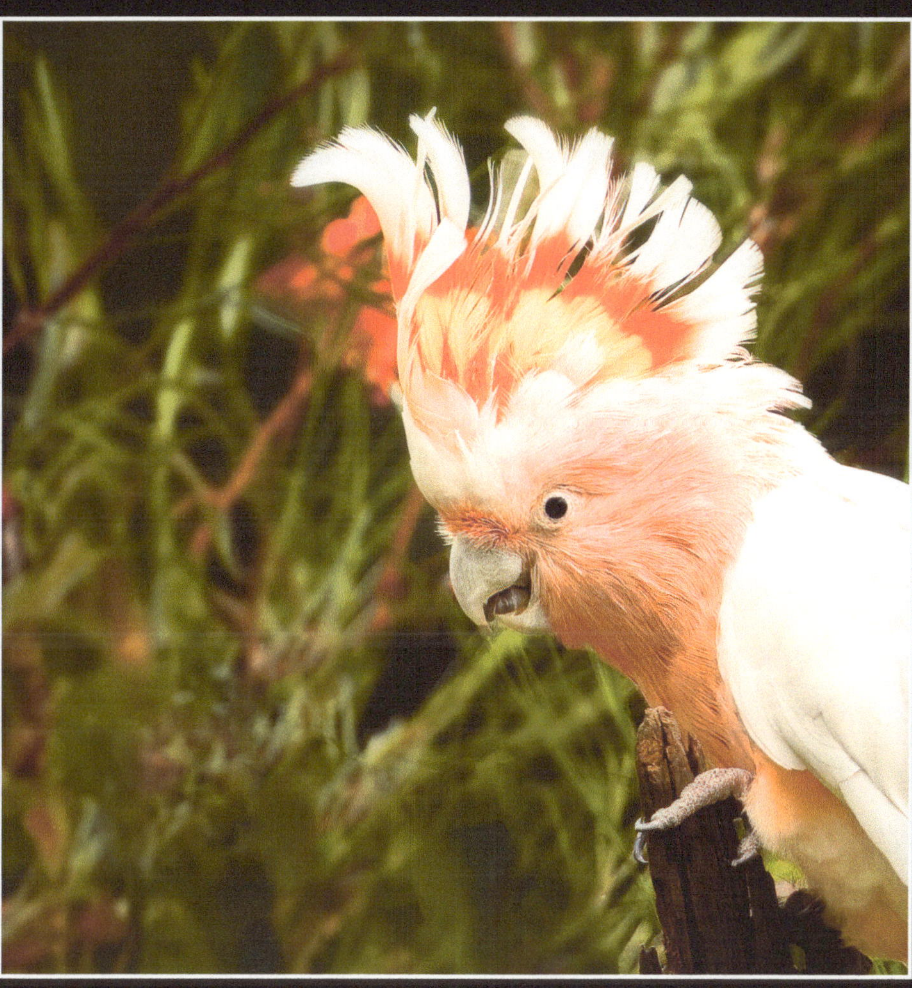

Major Mitchell's Cockatoo

Courage is not the absence of fear—
it's the decision that something else
is more important.

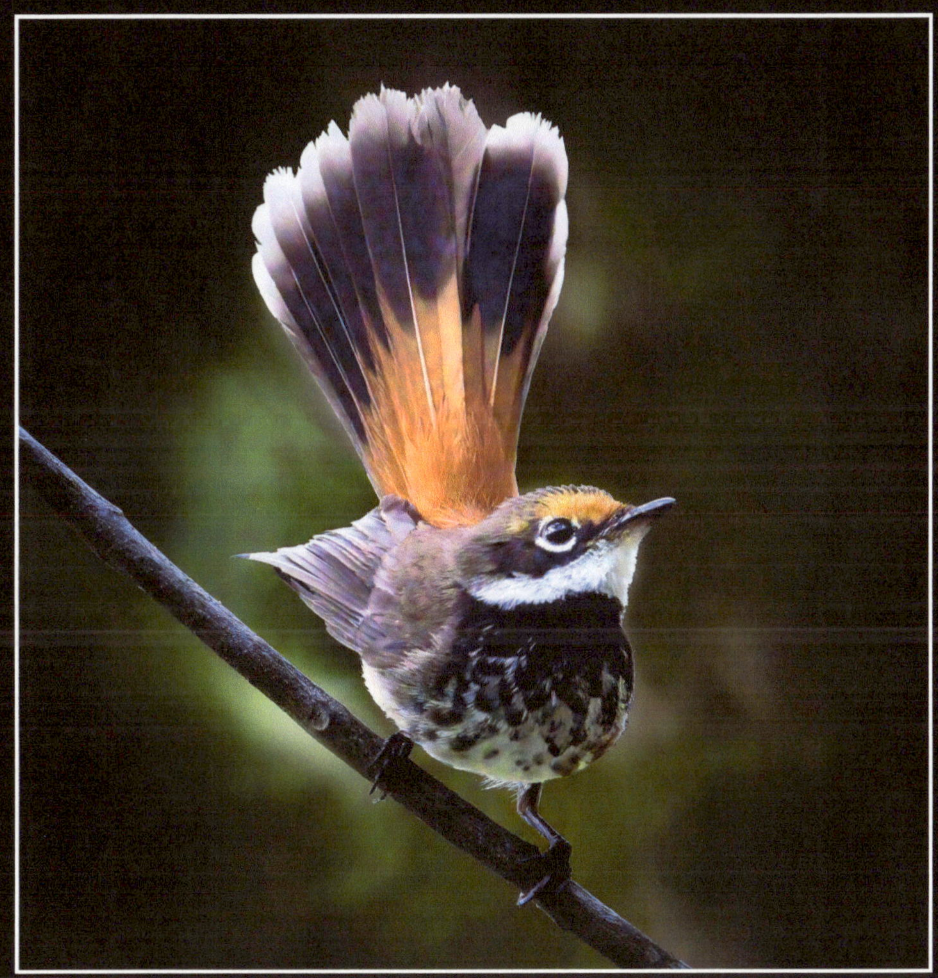

Rufous Fantail

You don't have to match to
belong together.
You don't have to be identical to
be perfect companions.
Sometimes the most beautiful bonds
celebrate our differences.

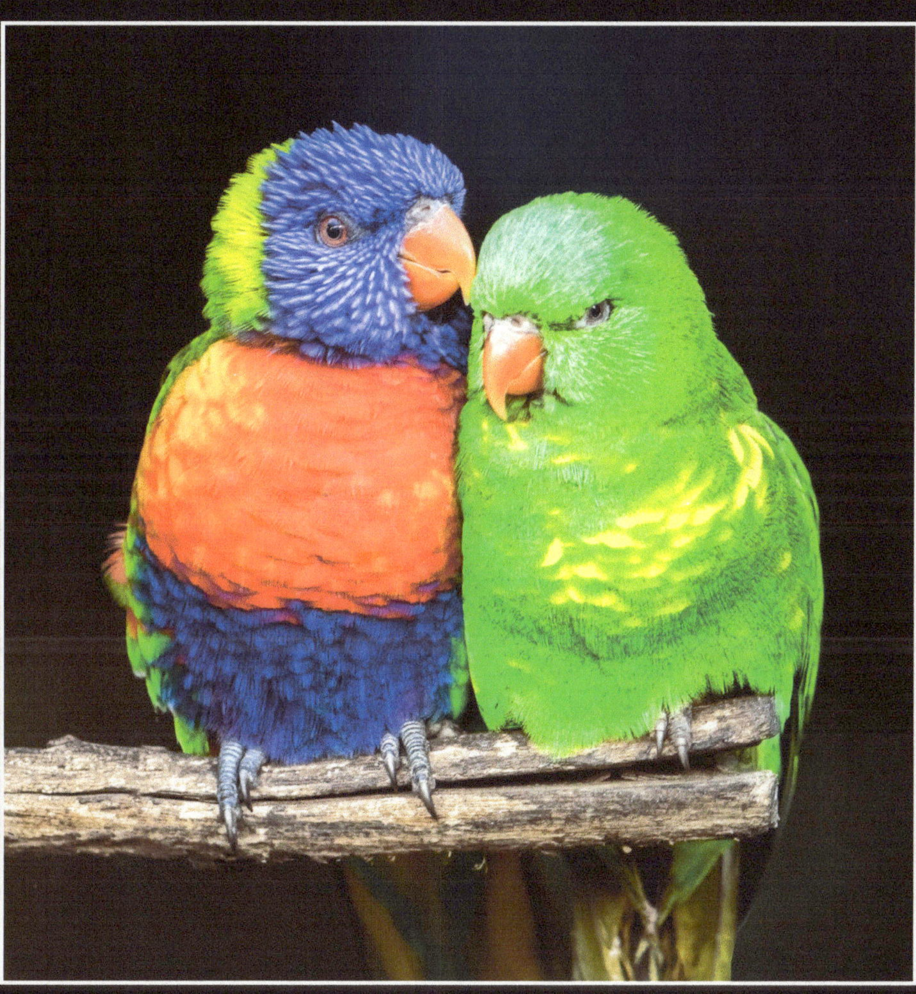

Rainbow and Scaly-breasted Lorikeet

We were never meant to
stay grounded.
We were meant to remember
that we have wings, and to
use them.

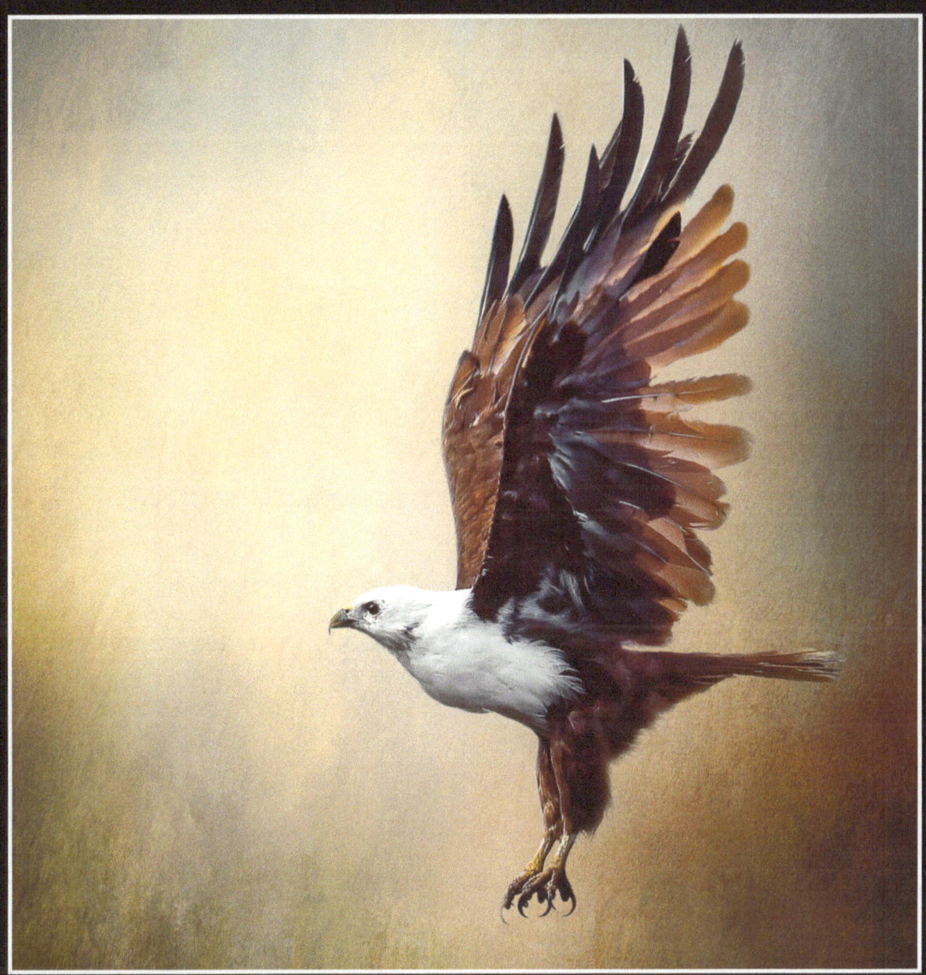

Brahminy Kite

Every deep breath calms your
nervous system.
Every mindful moment centers
your spirit.
Every conscious choice empowers
your journey.
Every present awareness heals
your soul.

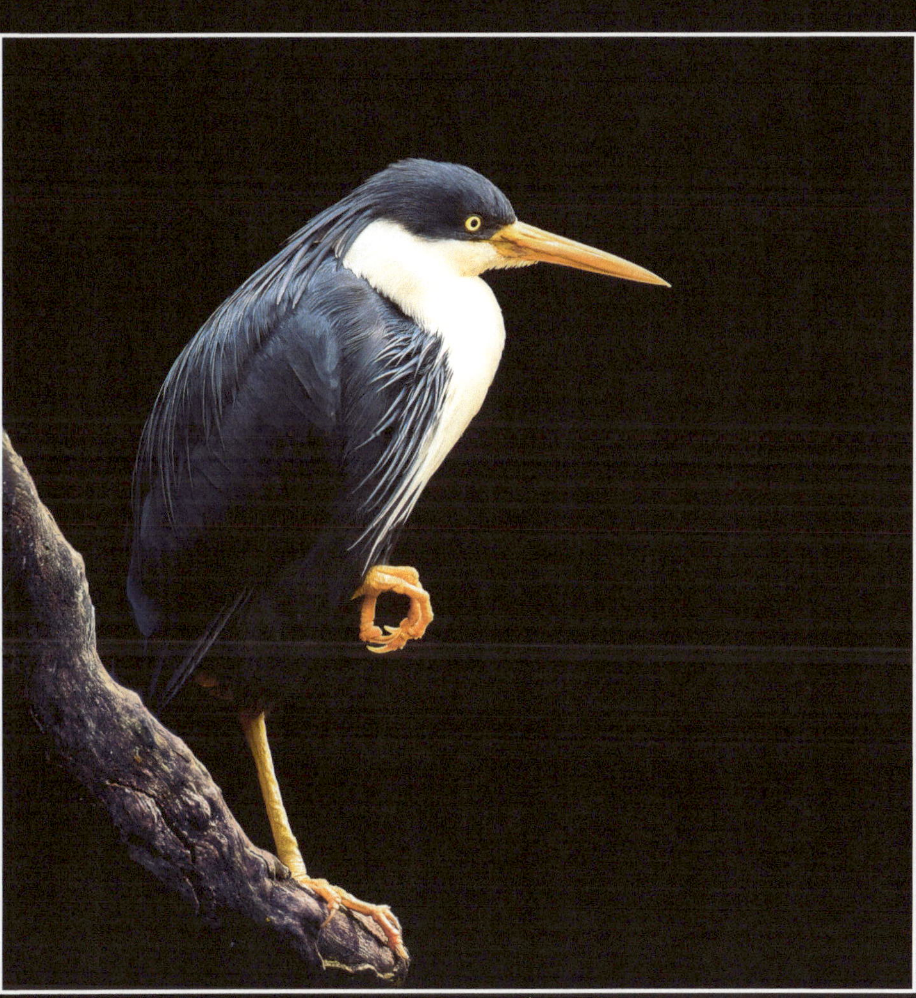

Pied Heron

Watching a pelican fish teaches us that success comes from combining patience with perfect timing.

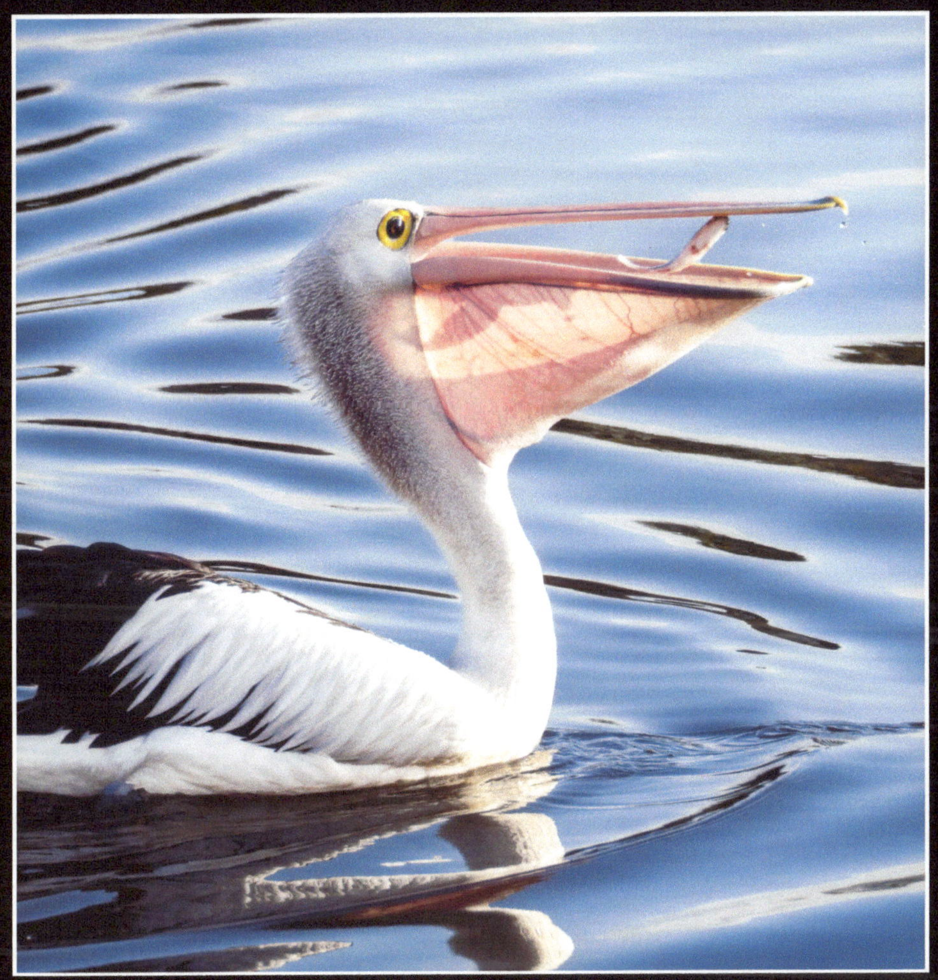

Pelican

Every bird that visits your home
brings a message of hope.
Every butterfly that crosses your path
carries beauty.
Every flower that blooms in your
garden offers joy.

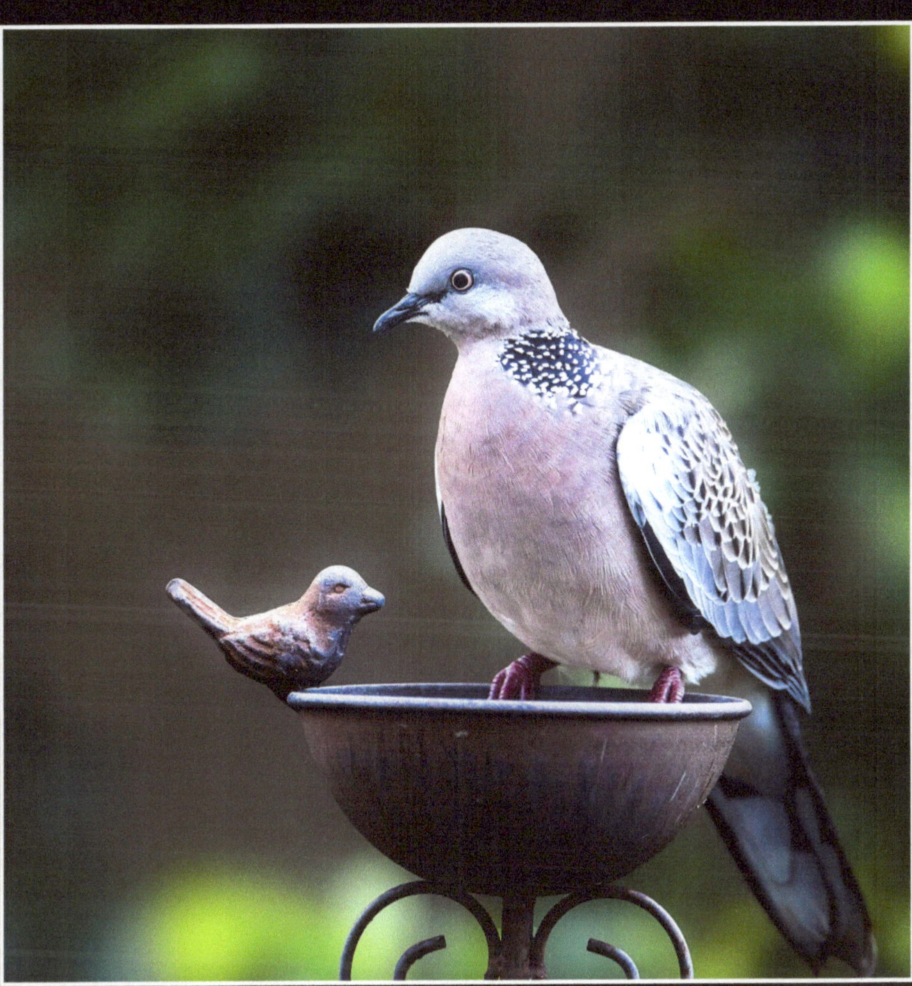

Spotted Dove

Wear your colors boldly,
carry yourself with dignity,
and remember that your presence
alone brightens the world.

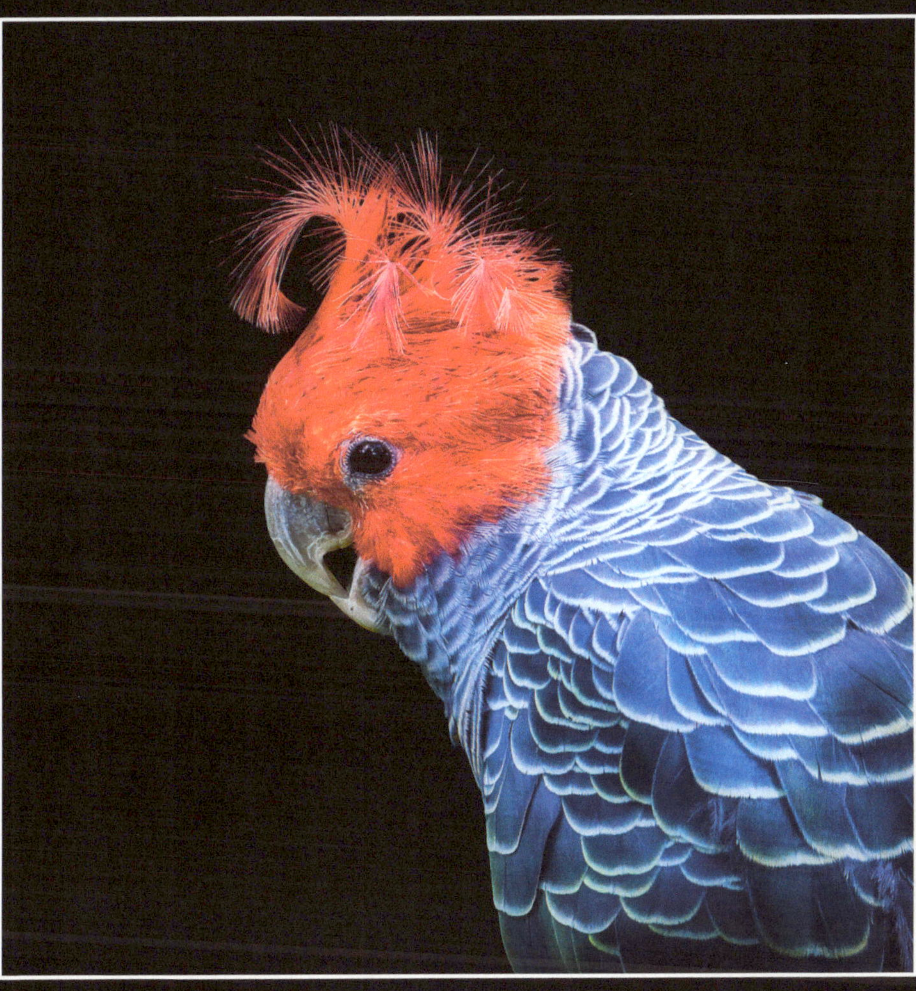

Gang Gang Cockatoo

The birds outside your window are
singing for you.
The breeze through the leaves is
breathing with you.
The sunlight on your face is
warming your spirit.
The earth beneath your feet is
supporting your journey.

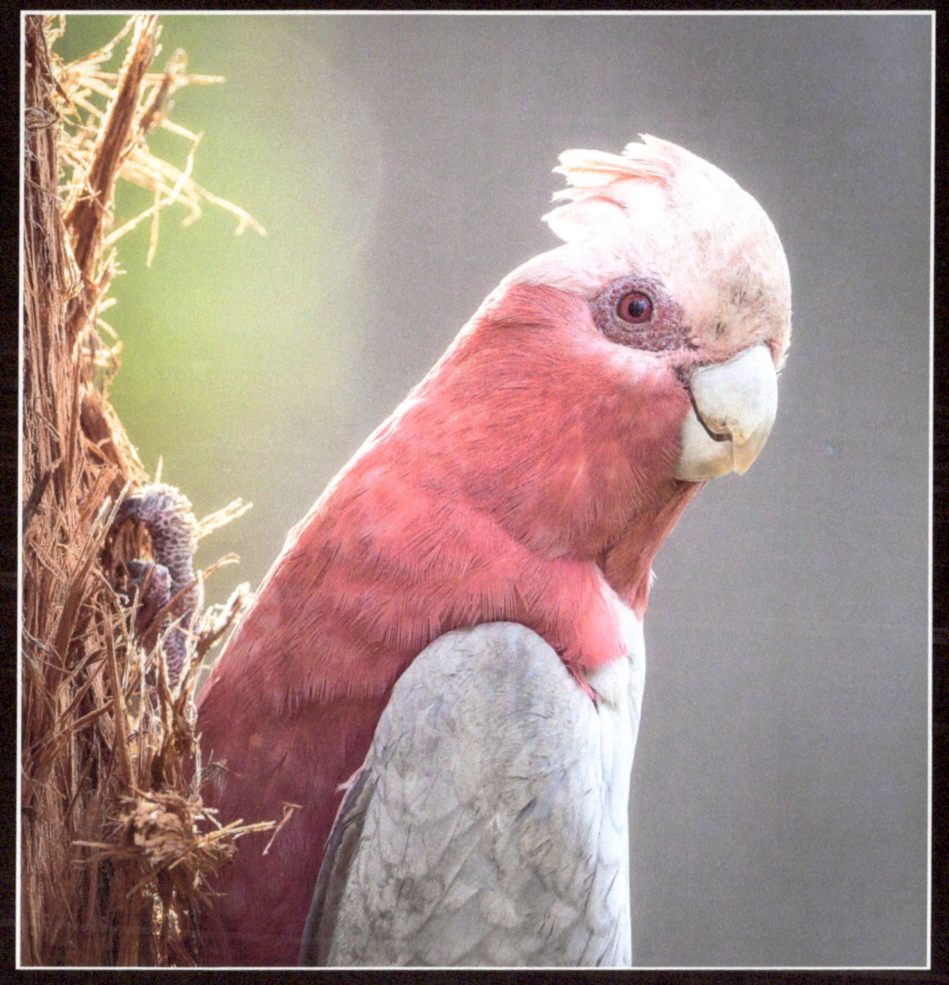

Galah

Every expert was once a beginner.
Every master was once a disaster.
Every giant was once someone taking
their very first wobbly steps.

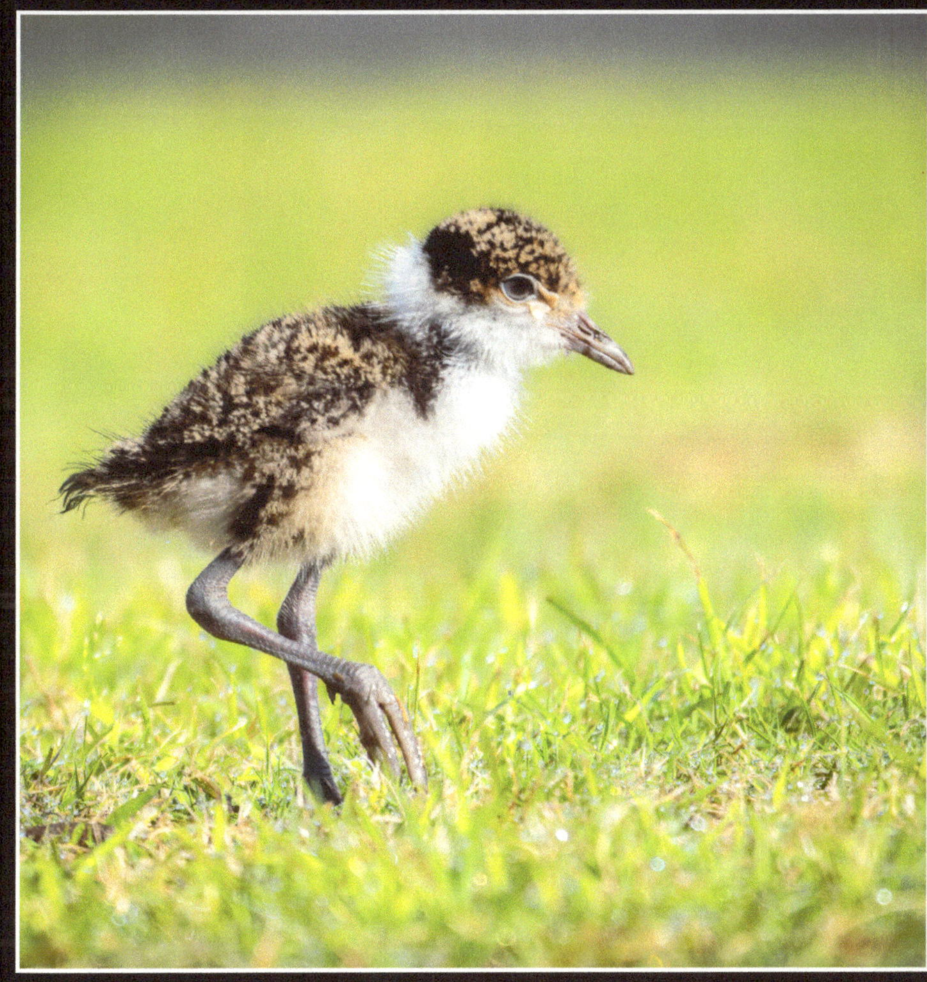

Masked Lapwing

Your sensitivity is not weakness.
Your emotions are not burdens.
Your caring is not foolishness.
Your heart is not too much.

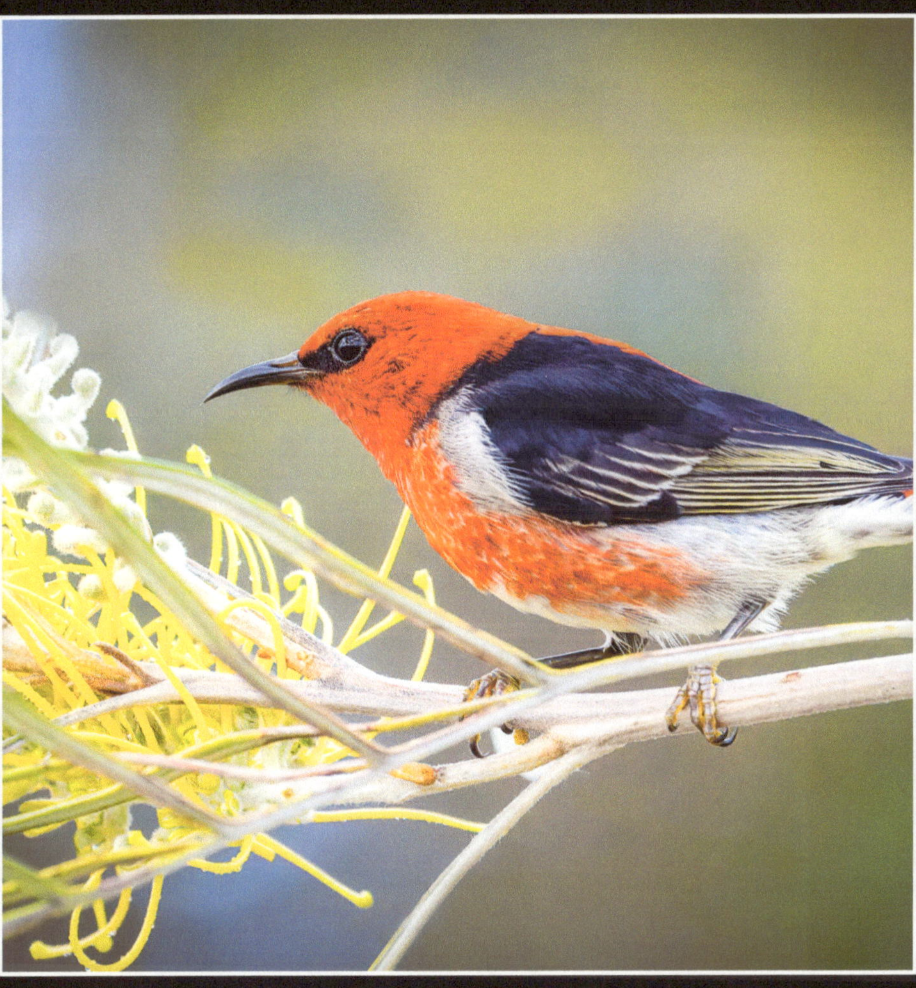

Scarlett Honeyeater

Real joy isn't about having everything—it's about finding complete satisfaction in whatever is in front of you right now.

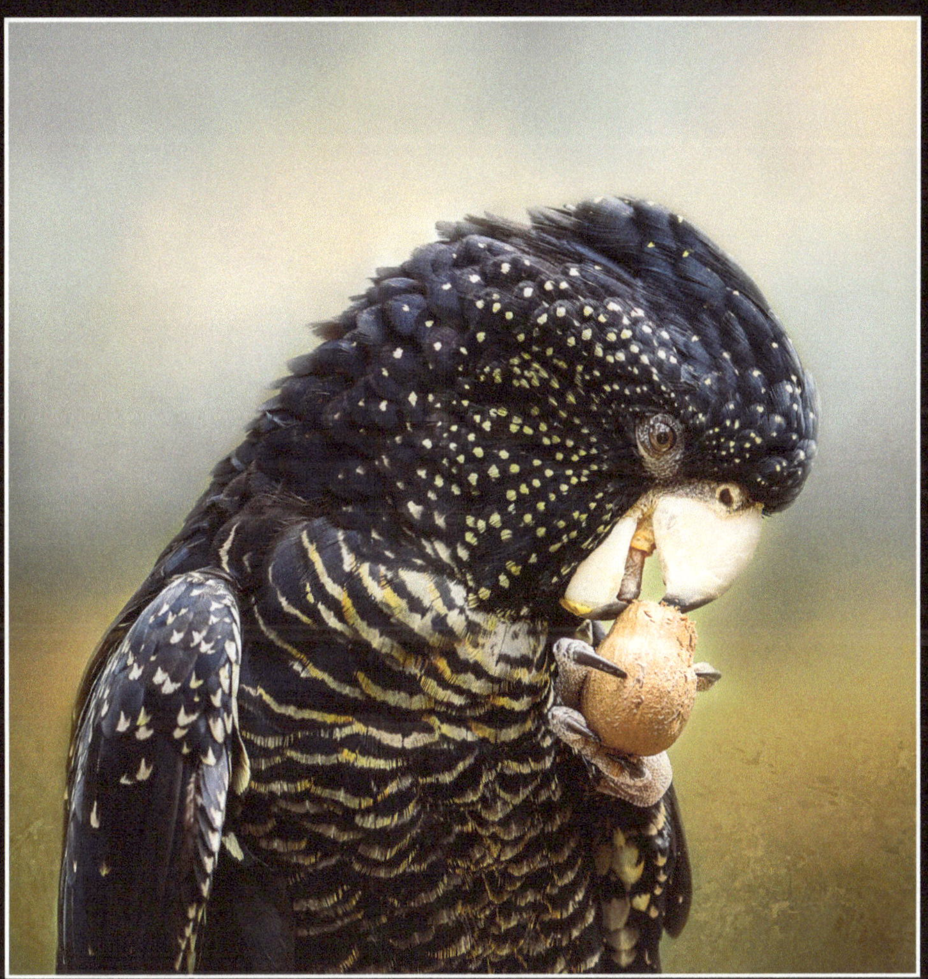

Red-tailed Black-Cockatoo

Life's sweetest rewards often come
to those who are patient enough
to wait,
and quick enough to act when the
moment arrives.

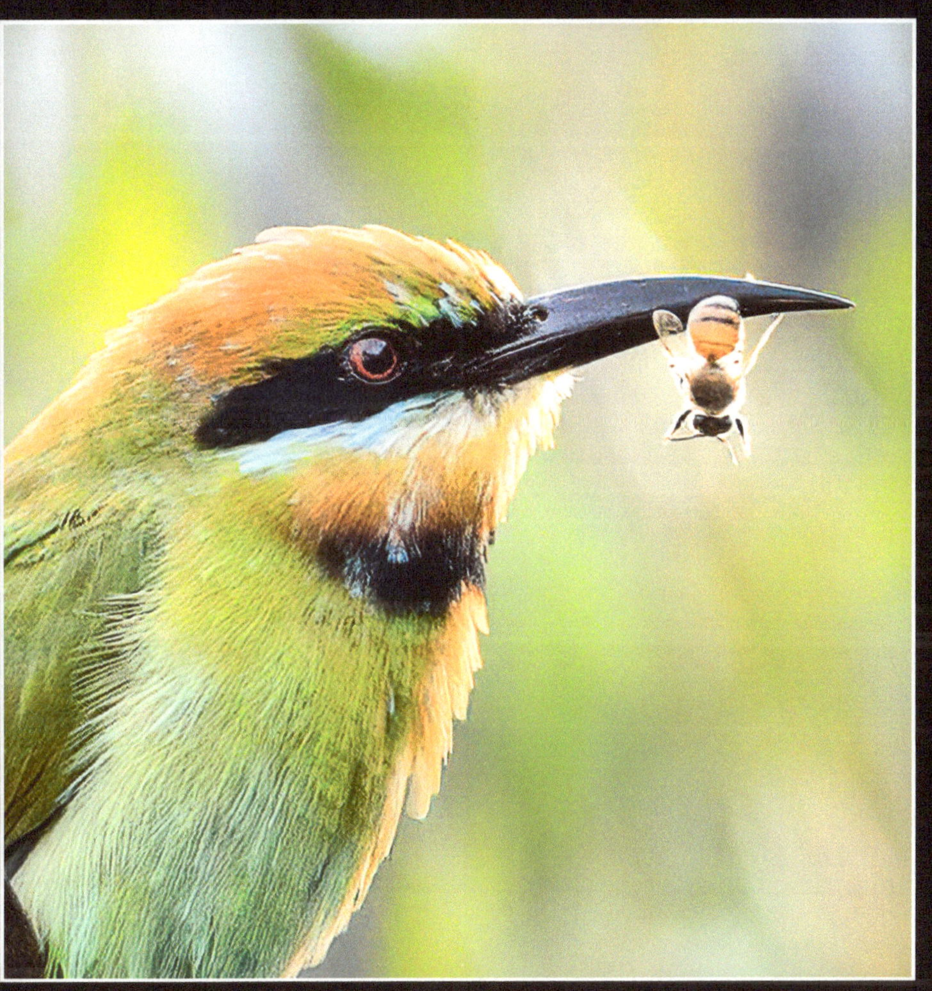

Rainbow Bee-eater

In the swan's devotion to its young,
we see that love's greatest expression
is consistent, caring presence.

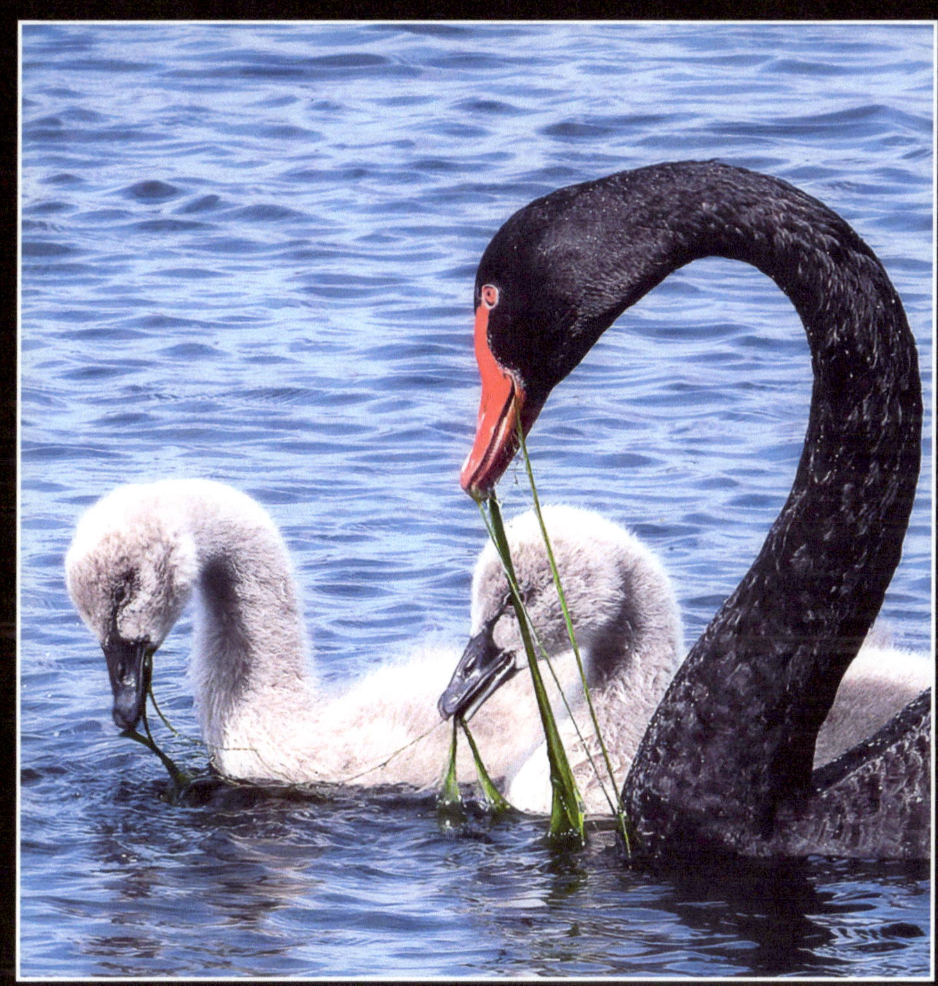

Black Swan

You are braver than you believe.
You are stronger than you feel.
You are more resilient than you realize.
You are more loved than you know.

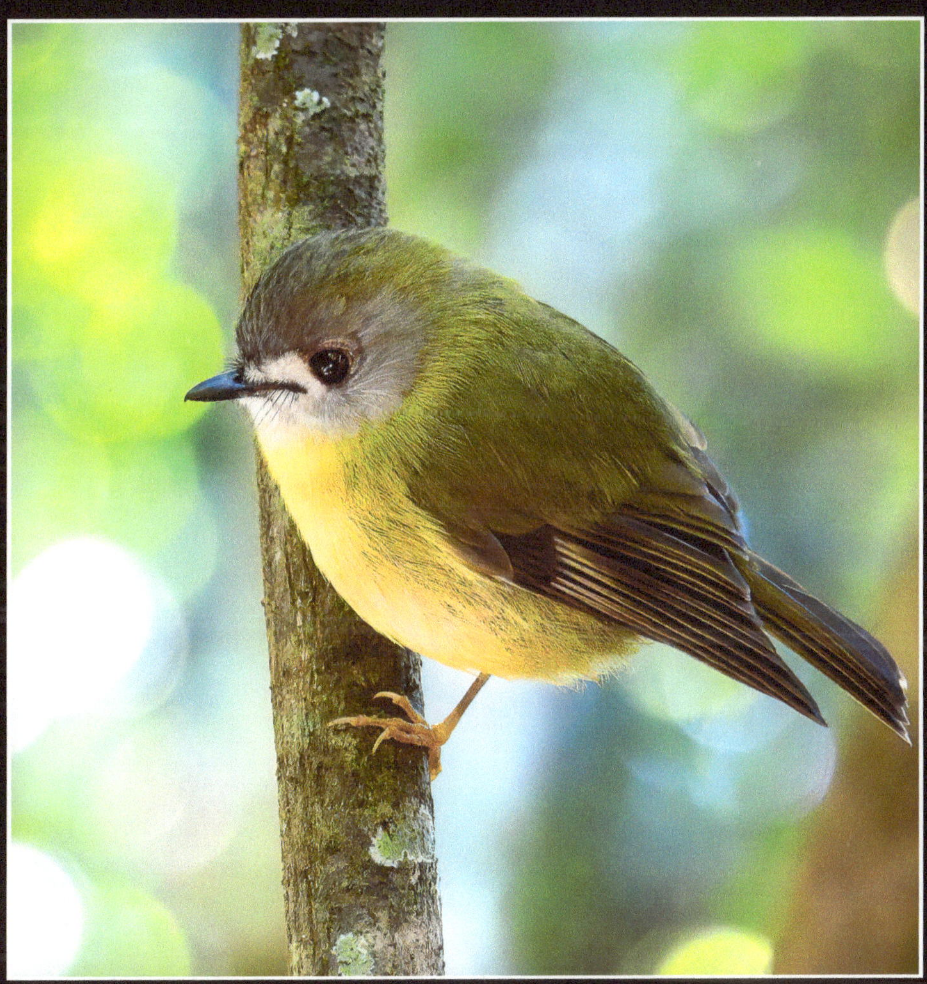

Pale-yellow Robin

You don't need to be big to make people smile — just be your round, fluffy, delightful self.

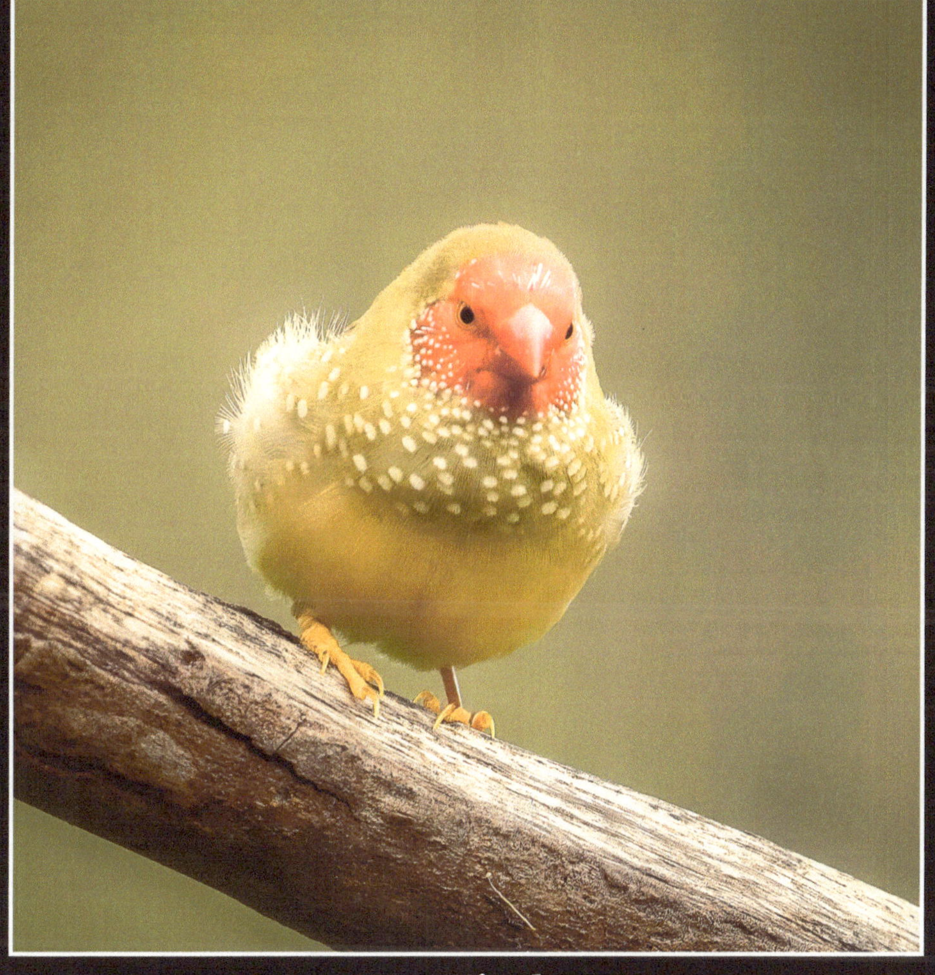

Star Finch

If you're going to chase dreams, do it with flair — and maybe a splash of extra wing color.

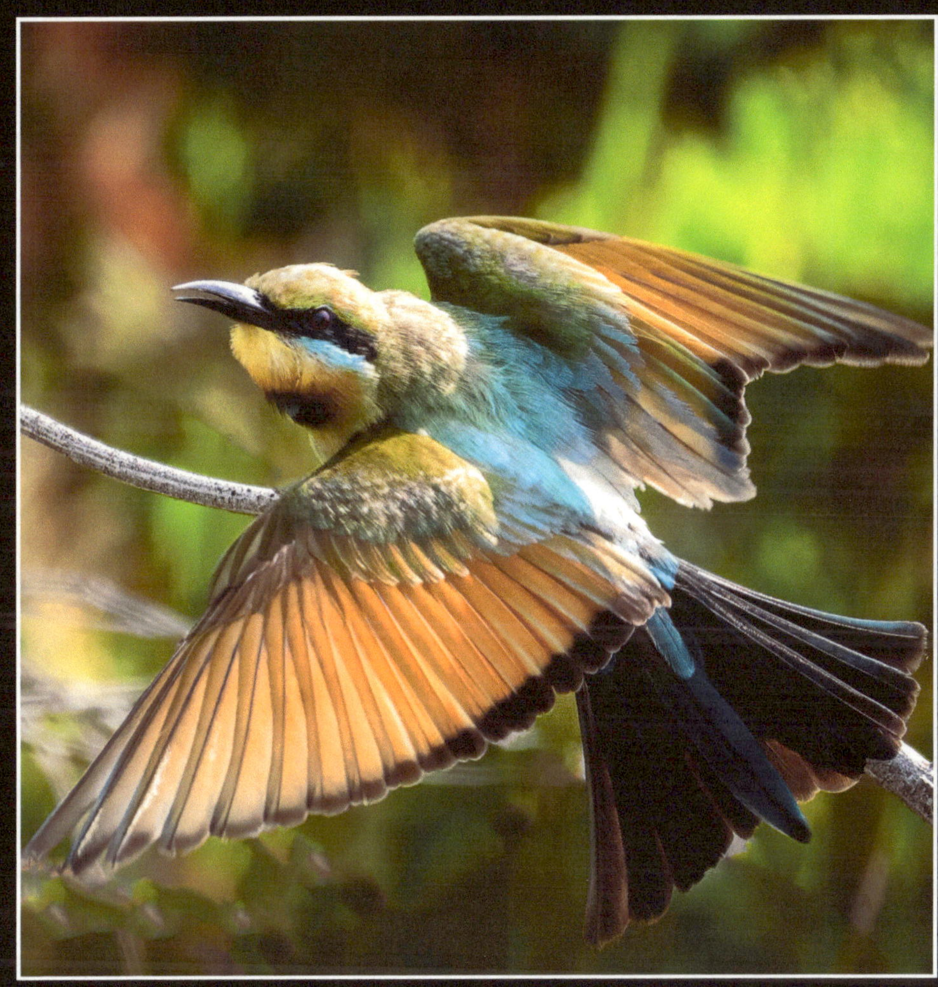

Rainbow Bee-eater

Never underestimate the healing
power of a good laugh!

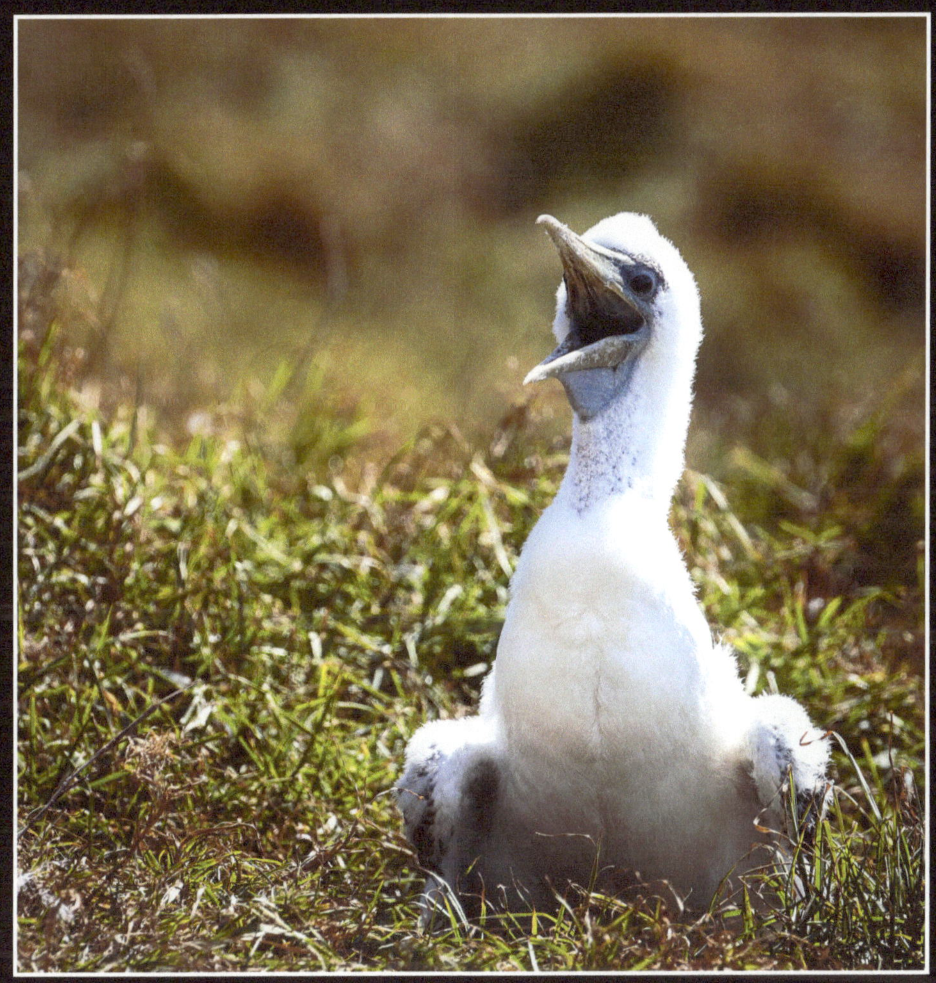

Masked Booby (Juvenile)

When was the last time you
stopped to watch a bird at rest?
What might its patience teach you?

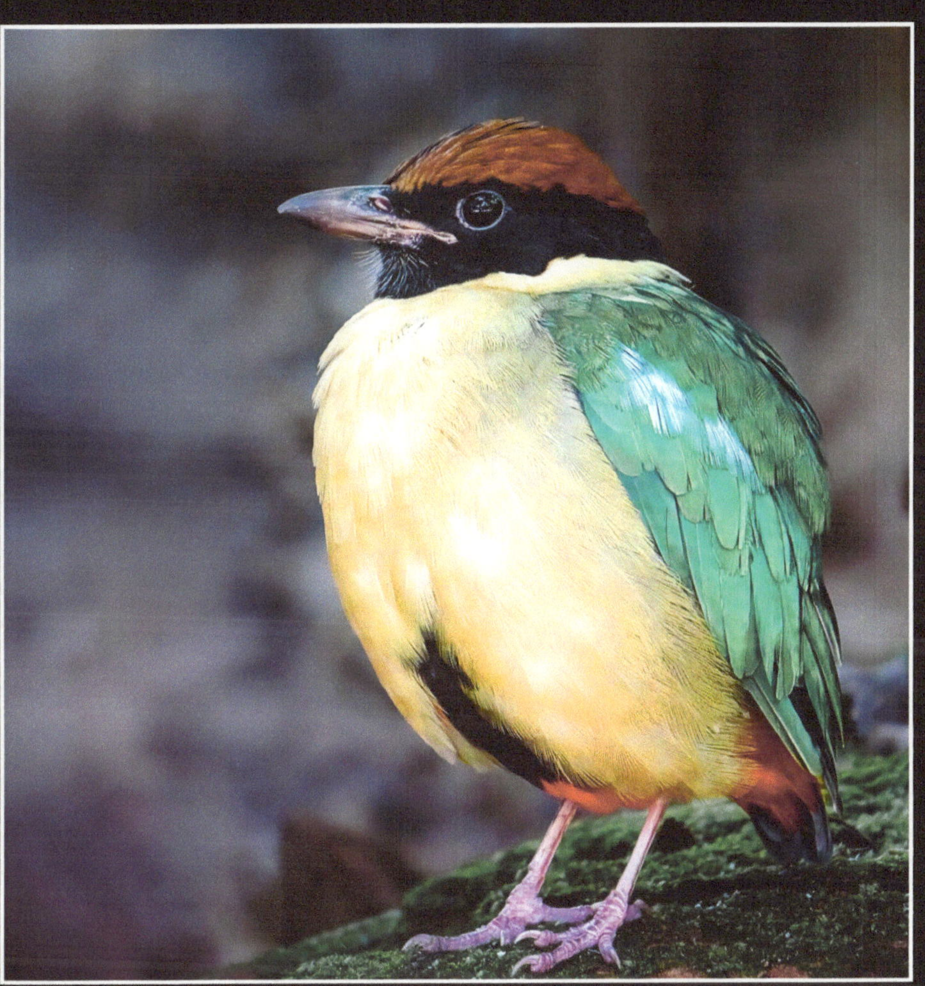

Noisy Pitta

The most beautiful creatures are those who've learned that their differences aren't flaws to hide, but gifts to celebrate.

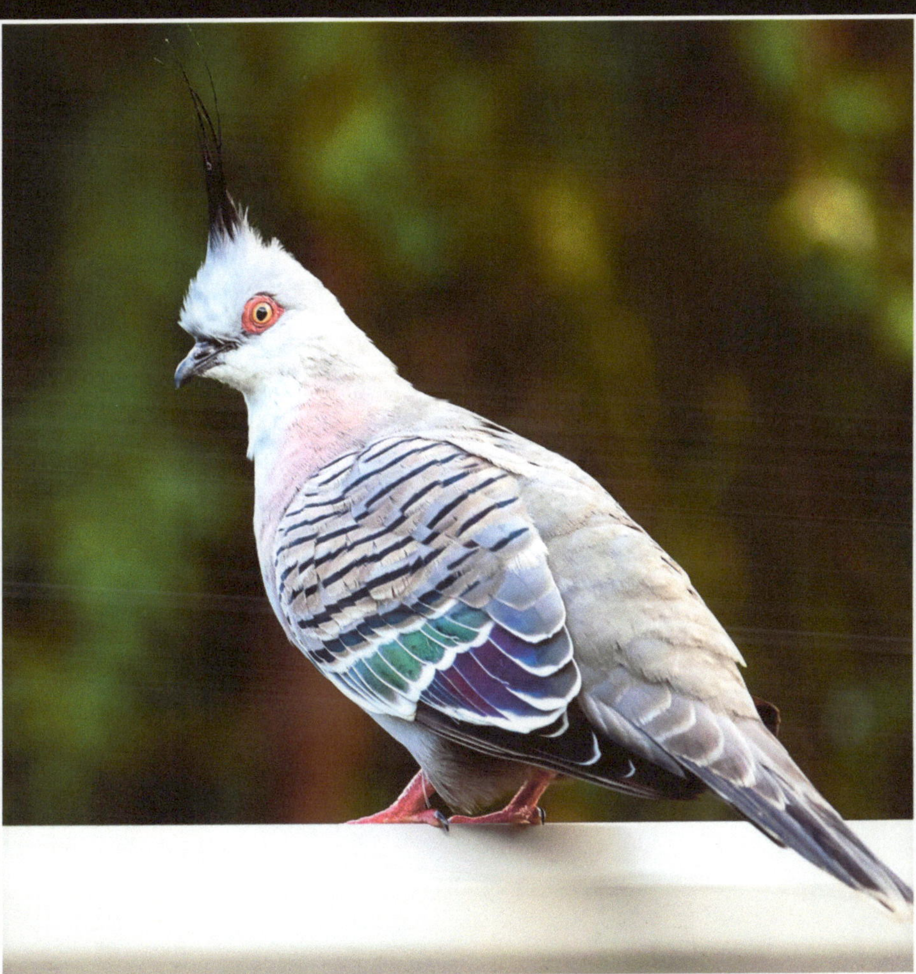

Crested Pigeon

Rest is not retreat— it is strategic positioning for the next adventure.

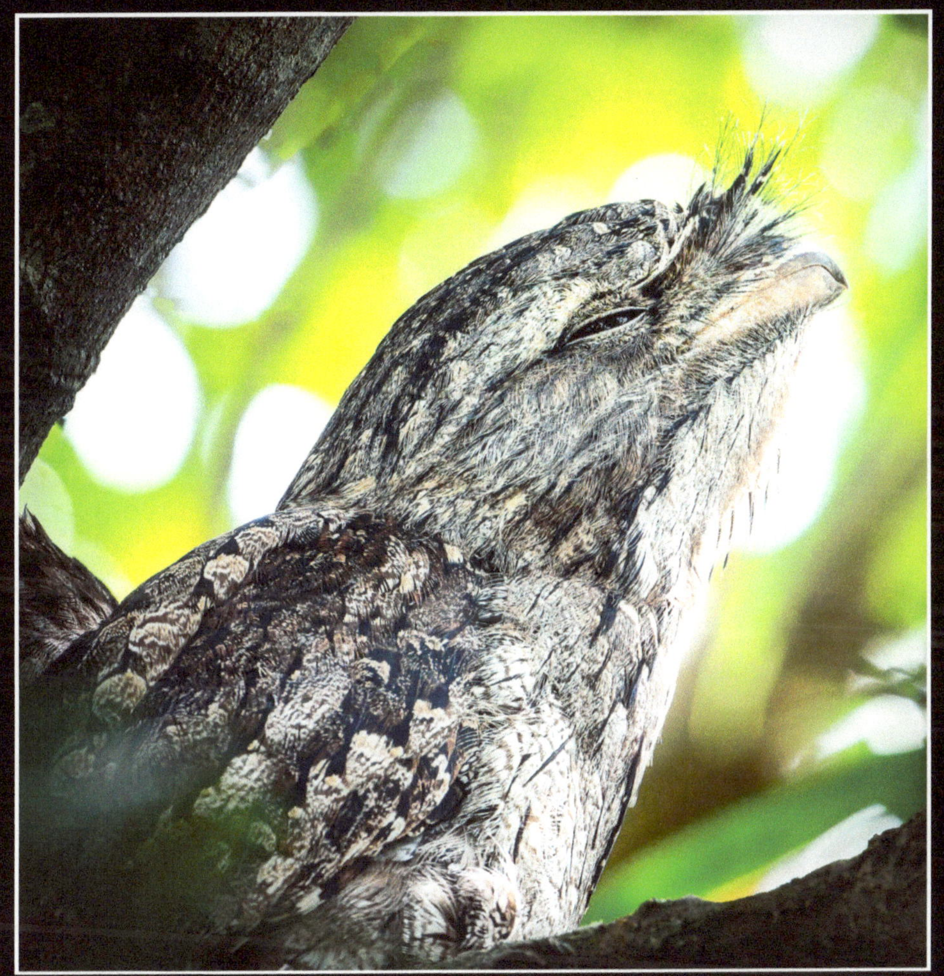

Tawny Frogmouth

Two truths about flight (and life):
First, you must trust what you
cannot see.
Second, you must trust what you
cannot control.

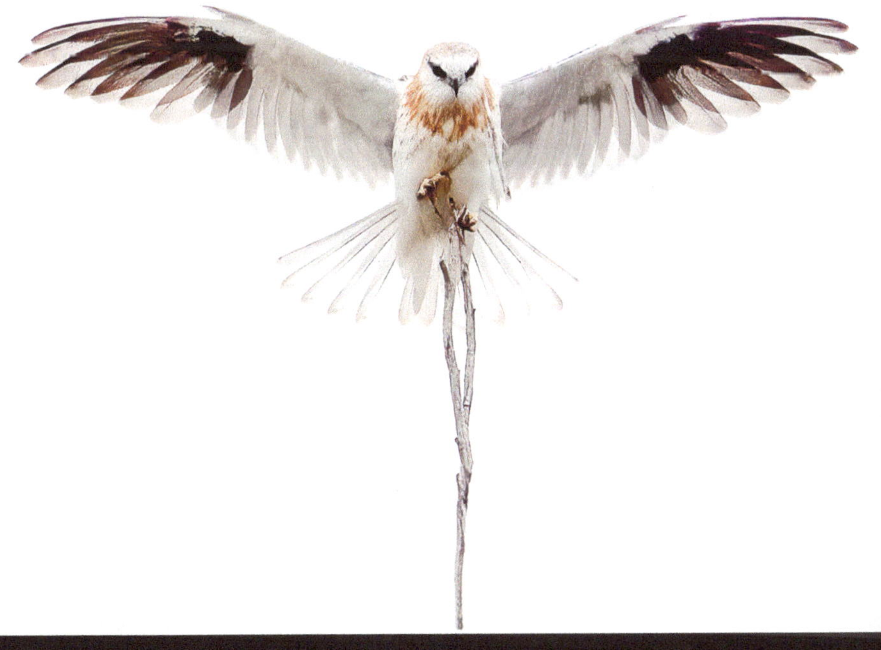

Black-shouldered Kite (Juvenile)

The trick to parenting — deep breaths,
short memories, and a good
sense of humour.

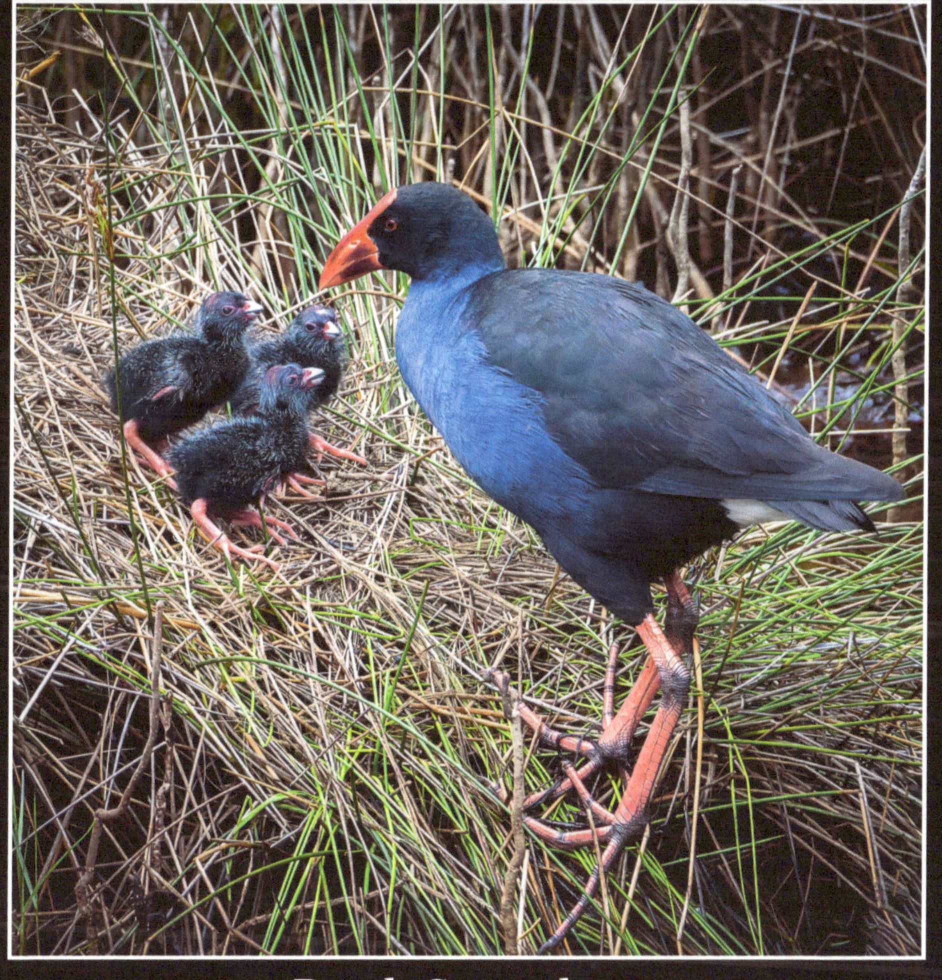

Purple Swamphen

Every bird that lands near you
brings a blessing.
Every song that reaches your ears
carries healing.
Every flight witnessed offers
inspiration.
Every moment spent in nature
nurtures your soul.

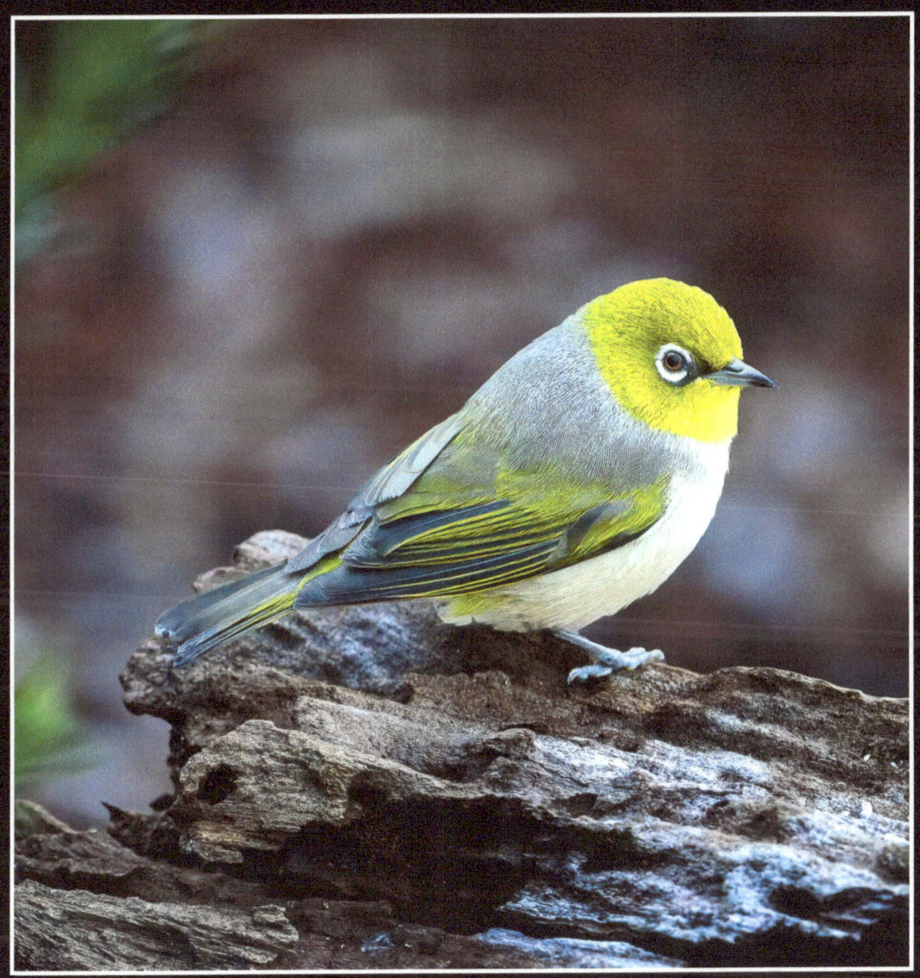

Silvereye

Wear your joy like this robin
wears yellow—boldly, naturally,
and without seeking anyone's
approval.

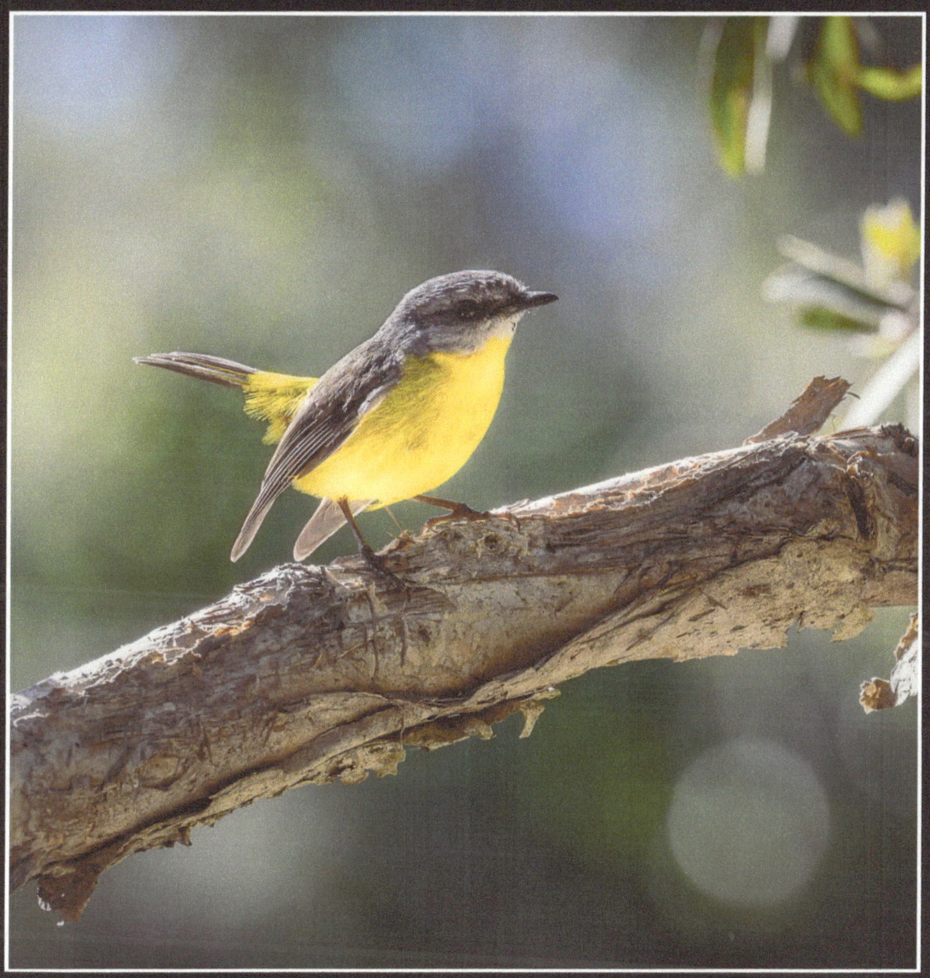

Eastern Yellow Robin

Listen closely — wisdom often
arrives disguised as silence.

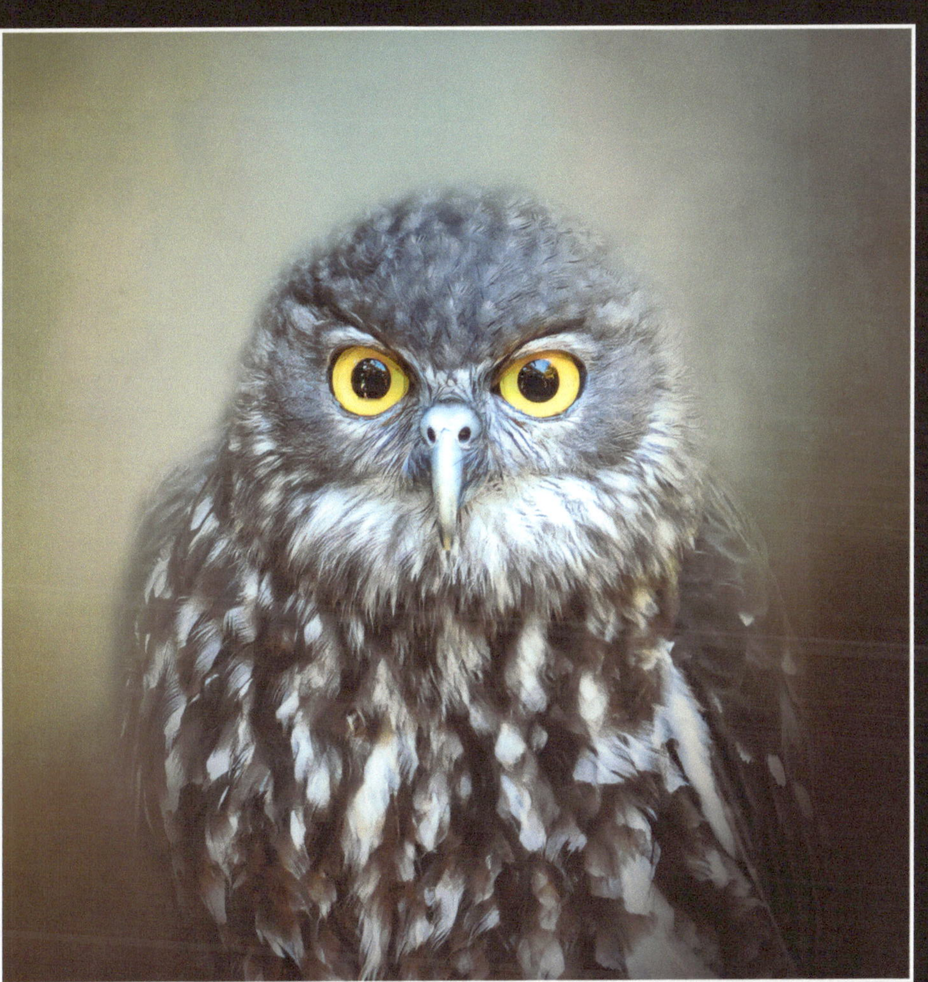

Barking Owl

If opportunity doesn't knock, fly
to the nearest tree and
help yourself.

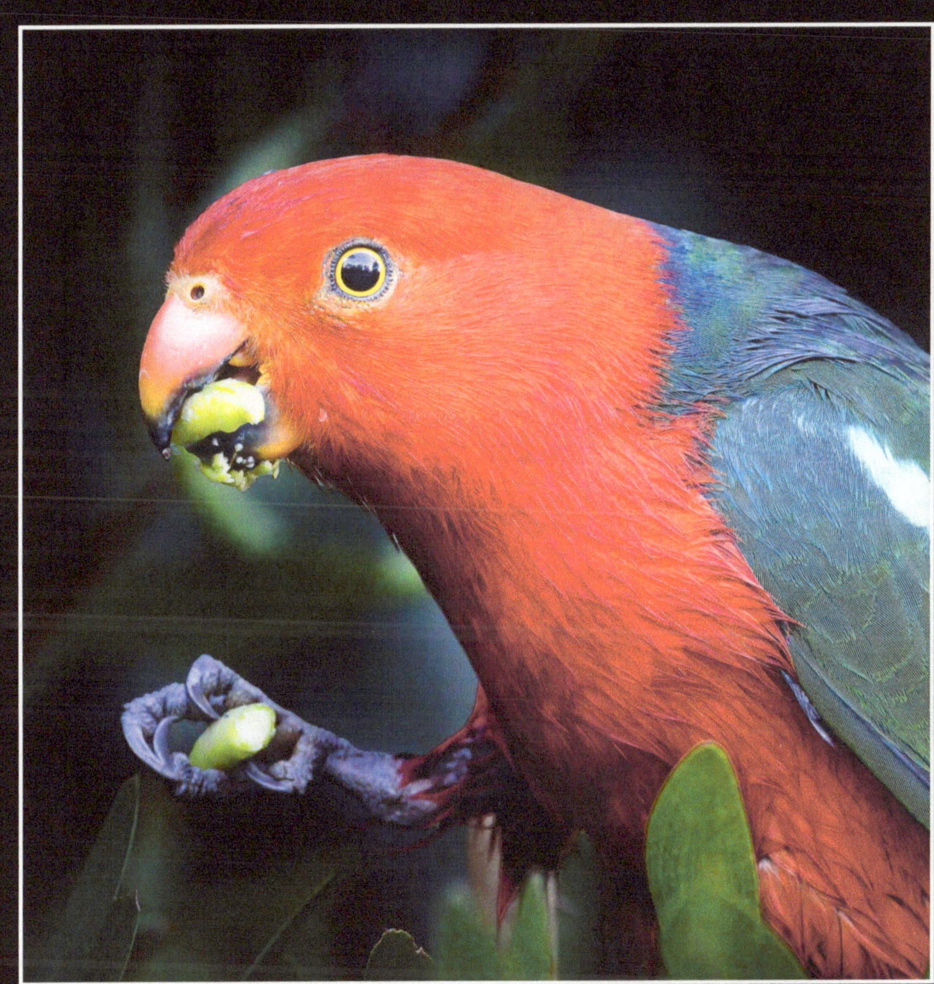

**King Parrot

Photographs and words by Julie Pallant (PhD)

All of the photographs in this book were captured by Julie Pallant, a photographer, digital artist, and author based in Ballina, a seaside town in northern NSW, Australia.

Julie's photographs were taken in her local area and celebrate the amazing variety of Australia's birdlife.

The quotes in this book were created as a gentle reminder of the healing power of the natural world.

Julie's career as a Psychologist, with a focus on stress, coping, and wellbeing, gave her a deep understanding of the challenges of modern life.

Want more information about the Australian birds featured in this book?

More information on each of the birds featured in the book, is available using the links provided at:

https://linktr.ee/jpallant